Polymer Clay Special Effects

A Beginner's Guide to Creating Unique Surface Designs and Beautiful Jewelry

LAUREN WALLACE

Quarto.com

First Published in 2025 by Quarry Books, an imprint of The Quarto Group,
100 Cummings Center, Suite 265-D, Beverly, MA 01915, USA.
T (978) 282-9590 F (978) 283-2742

Quarry Books titles are also available at discount for retail, wholesale, promotional, and bulk purchase. For details, contact the Special Sales Manager by email at specialsales@quarto.com or by mail at The Quarto Group, Attn: Special Sales Manager, 100 Cummings Center, Suite 265-D, Beverly, MA 01915, USA.

10 9 8 7 6 5 4 3 2 1

ISBN: 978-0-7603-9376-5

Digital edition published in 2025
eISBN: 978-0-7603-9377-2

Library of Congress Cataloging-in-Publication Data available

Design: Laura Klynstra
Cover Image: Glenn Scott Photography

Printed in China

Dedication

To the first boy I ever loved, your laughter still echoes in my memories. To the sibling who challenged me the most, your relentless spirit pushed me to grow in ways I never thought possible. To the friend who never judged me, thank you for holding space for my flaws and fears. To the man who lifted me up, your unwavering support has been my anchor. To the greatest captain and fisherman on Lake Ontario, your tales of the waters were enchanting and the way your eyes lit up with each story you shared will be on replay in my mind forever. To my very own Peter Pan, you brought magic into my life, reminding me that the spirit of youth never truly fades. Your belief in dreams inspired me to chase my own, no matter how impossible they seemed.

To the big brother I lost far too soon, the void you left is immeasurable. Your memory and presence is woven into every moment of my life, a bittersweet reminder of the love we shared.

Thank you, for every piece of our story. I will carry you with me *until world's end.*

Love you always in all ways.

Your little sister,
Lauren

In loving memory
Jeff R. Wallace II
April 24, 1995–July 22, 2022

piccassio
Alcohol Ink
VIOLET
B034
piccassio
Alcohol Ink
SAPPHIRE
B035
0.35 fl oz (10ml)
piccassio
Alcohol Ink
BLUE GREEN
B039
piccassio
Alcohol Ink
WHITE
HIGH DENSITY
B022
0.35 fl oz (10ml)

Contents

Introduction

Before We Begin: A Mindset to Explore

For me, art has always been an escape. A way to disconnect from the pressures of this world. An opportunity to release the emotions held tightly inside and alchemize them into something beautiful and tangible.

I didn't know I was going to fall in love with polymer clay—it's funny to think one could fall in love with something like that at all—but I have, and I'll explain why. Starting from a simple block, polymer clay becomes a blank canvas, and its transformation holds infinite potential. There's no wrong way with this medium. It's malleable, adapts well, and is incredibly forgiving. Maybe it's silly to consider this medium a friend, but sometimes in life we need something that'll change and evolve gracefully alongside us. As you begin this journey with me, I want you, my friend, to know this art is a safe space.

The goal of this book isn't only to give you the knowledge and tools to expand your polymer clay skills, but also to encourage the ability to believe in the power of your own creativity. Within you lies a wellspring of untapped potential.

Polymer Clay Special Effects is designed to inspire and walk you through the fundamental techniques of working with polymer clay—from shaping and conditioning the clay to creating intricate designs and adding stunning finishes. Through easy-to-follow instructions, helpful tips, and inspiring examples, you'll learn the basics, which will help you to understand how to manipulate polymer clay with precision and finesse. Soon, you'll be turning these simple shapes and techniques into stunning and intricate designs. Then together we'll walk through techniques that can capture the galaxy, or that will result in a stone that looks so real you might begin to question its authenticity. This book is meant to provide a better understanding of this medium and move you forward in your polymer clay journey with confidence, whether you're a beginner or an experienced artist.

As you embark on this path, remember that great art isn't created overnight, but rather through a process of continual growth and exploration. Allow yourself the grace to embrace the journey. Let this book serve as a compass, directing you toward new techniques, perspectives, and approaches that'll ignite your creativity and expand your artistic horizons. There is freedom in this art, and I hope you find it here.

The Fundamentals

This chapter explores the different types of polymer clay available, essential tools for beginners, basic techniques for shaping and sculpting, and important tips for curing that will help you embark on your creative journey with confidence.

Polymer Clay 101

Polymer clay is a versatile and popular material used in crafting, sculpting, and jewelry making. It's a type of modeling clay that hardens when baked in an oven, making it durable and long lasting. It was first created in the 1930s by a German doll maker who was searching for a modeling clay that could be cured at home to create flexible dolls. It's amazing how something as popular as polymer clay could have such a personal history.

Polymer clay is a type of synthetic modeling material composed of polyvinyl chloride particles. When the polymer clay is heated, its particles soften and fuse together, creating the signature durable and flexible material we all know. When the clay is being cured, it undergoes a process known as *polymerization*, where the molecules in the clay rearrange to form a stable and solid material.

Why use polymer clay for jewelry? The answer is simple: Polymer clay is incredible. It's durable, flexible, versatile, and lightweight. All of these are qualities that make any earring lover very, very happy.

Measurement Lingo

Polymer clay blocks often come with lines dividing them into fourths. Instead of measuring out clay in ounces or grams, I'll use those handy lines and other simple terms to describe how much clay to use. I just don't work in weighed-out amounts. Part of the reason polymer clay is so amazing is because there is so much freedom and wiggle room to adjust it to your liking!

- **Block.** Generally speaking, each block of clay is about 1.5 to 2 ounces (43–56 g).
- **Dice.** Imagine dicing a tomato or onion into pebble-sized bits.
- **Dime.** Crafters in the US will be familiar with the rough size of a dime, but if you're living in another part of the world, aim for a round disk of clay about ¾ inch (18 mm) across.
- **Part.** A part is a quarter of a block, approximately 0.4 to 0.5 ounces (11–14 g) each. A recipe could call for 1 part, 2 parts, or more.
- **Quarter.** This is another coin that US crafters will know. If you're living in another part of the world, aim for a round disk of clay about 1 inch (2.5 cm) across.

Safety

Polymer clay is generally considered a nontoxic material when used as intended and properly cured. Most commercial brands are safe for crafting and modeling. Although it's a nontoxic material, certain precautions should be taken to ensure safe use:

- Avoid ingestion.
- Use ventilation when baking.
- Avoid burning the clay, as the fumes can be harmful. See also page 110 in the Curing and Finishing chapter.

Polymer Clay Brands

There are several popular brands of polymer clay available, offering a variety of colors, formulations, and features for artists. Some of the well-known brands that we'll be using in this book include:

- **Sculpey.** My personal favorite! Sculpey is one of the most recognized brands of polymer clay. There are a range of clay types to explore.
    - **Liquid Sculpey.** This is a versatile liquid polymer clay that can be used for various techniques, but acts as a great adhesive when creating jewelry with polymer clay. It's available in both opaque and translucent colors.
    - **Sculpey III.** A soft and easy-to-work-with polymer clay, Sculpey III is ideal for beginners and experienced artists.
    - **Sculpey Premo.** This premium polymer clay line by Sculpey is known for its strength, flexibility, and durability. It holds fine details well.
    - **Sculpey Soufflé.** It's a lightweight and airy polymer clay that is perfect for creating jewelry and other delicate projects. Soufflé has a suede-like finish and comes in a range of unique colors.
- **Cernit.** A European brand of clay that's becoming more popular worldwide, Cernit offers a range of unique colors and special-effects clay, including translucent, metallic, and pearlescent options. Cernit clay is recognized for its strength and durability; it maintains its shape well and withstands wear over time. It's a clay that is suitable for many applications and can be combined with other materials and techniques to achieve creative results.
- **Staedtler FIMO.** A very consistent and high-quality clay, FIMO is a popular choice among polymer clay artists. FIMO has a variety of formulations and colors, and has great strength, durability, workability, and versatility. It's offered in a range of formulations, such as FIMO Soft, FIMO Leather-Effect, FIMO Professional, and FIMO Effect. Each of these has its own set of unique characteristics that are fun and interesting to explore.
- **Kato Polyclay.** Known for its excellent workability and vibrant colors, Kato Polyclay is a brand favored by many professional artists. It's a clay that takes more time when conditioning, but ends in great results. Kato also released a formula called Kato Soft to shorten the conditioning time.

Tip

Cernit translucent white, in my experience, stays the whitest and clearest after baking. No yellowing!

SOUFFLÉ
NUMBER ONE
Pâte polymère opaque
Opaque polymer clay
Opake Polymermasse
Pasta Polimerica opaca
Arcilla polimérica opaca
CERNIT
TRANSLUCENT
Pâte polymère translucide
Translucent polymer clay
Transluzente Polymermasse
Pasta Polimerica traslucida
Arcilla polimérica translúcida
STAEDTLER
FIMO
PROFESSIONAL
Modelliermasse
Modelling Clay
Pâte à modeler
Pasta de modelar
57 g (2 oz) e
FIMO
LEATHER EFFECT
CERNIT
TRANSLUCENT
STAEDTLER
FIMO
SOFT
57 g (2 oz) e
FIMO
LEATHER EFFECT
CERNIT
TRANSLUCENT
Sculpey
PREMO
2 oz (57 g)
Sculpey
SOUFFLÉ
1.7 oz (48 g)
Sculpey
SOUFFLÉ
1.7 oz (48.2 g)
Sculpey
PREMO
2 oz (57 g)
2 oz (57 g)

Essential Tools & Supplies

- **Handheld Rotary Tool (A).** A handheld rotary tool, like a Dremel, will allow you to sand and drill your clay pieces with precision and ease.
- **Acrylic Roller (B).** This is essential for rolling out polymer clay to a uniform thickness or smoothness.
- **Tissue Blades (C).** Used to cut clean edges on your slab or slice your canes, a tissue blade is an essential in this art.
- **Cutters (D).** Available in various shapes and sizes, these are useful for cutting out precise shapes and designs from polymer clay. To see more about two of my favorite cutter suppliers, see pages 20–21.
- **Extruder (E).** This tool is used to make forms and coils with clay. The clay passes through the column with applied pressure.
- **Clay Tools (F–I).** These tools have a variety of uses, such as sculpting and precise detailing.
- **Precision Knife (J).** This tool will come in handy with pretty much everything as you become more experienced with clay. From hand-cutting pieces to trimming edges, it's a very useful tool.
- **Sculpting Needle (K).** A stainless-steel sculpting needle is useful for sculpting flowers and adding details to your sculpted pieces.
- **Pliers (L).** These are used to assemble your jewelry.
- **Surface.** Working on an easy-to-clean, nonstick surface is essential. Two surfaces I recommend are tile and marble.
- **Clay Machine.** Otherwise known as a pasta maker, this will allow you to condition your clay and roll out a uniform thickness.
- **Liquid Clay.** This product can act as a bond. See also page 16.
- **Oven.** You can use your kitchen oven or source a tabletop oven if you want to keep your clay separate from your cooking (totally up to you, as long as you don't burn the clay). Baking polymer clay is an essential step in curing and hardening it.
- **Baking Sheet and Parchment Paper.** It's best to have a baking sheet specifically for your clay pieces. Parchment paper will keep the clay from sticking to the tray.

Tip

There are some great bundles of beginner tools for sale online. A simple search for beginner polymer clay tools may provide all of what you need.

A
B
C
D
H
I
G
F
D
E
J
K
L
D

Featured Tool: Cutters

There are many places to source different tools for your polymer clay journey. I just want to let you in on some of the best-kept secrets! I have sought out and tried so many different brands; here are two that are simply unbeatable.

Cutterly Designs

Cutterly Designs was founded by Diana and Cesar Andrade in 2020. It is a family-owned business based in Dallas, Texas, specializing in crafting high-quality cutters, each meticulously hand-drawn by Diana and 3D printed in their home office using 100% eco-friendly recycled filament. Their cutters feature a cozy round pressing surface that makes them easier to use. Cesar's engineering skills provide top-notch quality cutters featuring Diana's creative designs, making it the perfect partnership. They also offer texture plates to add intricate details to your projects. Find their shop at www.etsy.com/shop/cutterlydesigns.

Boldrady

Betty Kuttelwascher is the artist behind Boldrady, located in Switzerland. She was originally a screen printer, but left that career after discovering her passion for polymer clay and designing unique cutters. With fine attention to the structure of the cutter, Betty has created a product that doesn't hurt your hand during use. The thin, sharp cutting edge is meticulously designed to leave clean edges, but it's also durable. Betty draws all of her own designs. Betty is looking forward to the evolution of her designs in the months to come. You can find her items on www.etsy.com/shop/boldrady.

Jewelry Hardware & Findings

Though the hardware may seem like an afterthought, creating high-quality jewelry pieces requires good bones. The hardware is what holds the pieces together and what makes the jewelry wearable.

There are many types of hardware and findings you can source to finish your pieces. Jump rings are the circular findings that link each piece together in jewelry. Gold-plated rings are affordable and great for practice. These findings are known to tarnish over time, but are definitely more beginner friendly. As an experienced artist, I use gold-filled findings. These are much more expensive, but don't tarnish. If you're confident in sourcing the more expensive jump rings, you can also source sterling silver that'll withstand wear as well. The same goes for ear wires (fish hooks) that hook through your ear. Beginners may prefer to start with a less expensive option and eventually source gold or sterling silver hardware.

When you make a stud earring, you'll need to attach a post. I recommend using surgical-grade stainless steel posts as they're sturdy, durable, and hypoallergenic.

Tip

Throughout this book, you'll see charm findings that finish off an earring with a special touch. Charms and connectors can often complement a piece without adding too much weight.

Color Basics

Color theory is an essential aspect of art and design, providing a framework for understanding how colors interact and combine. When it comes to working with polymer clay, mastering color mixing can significantly enhance your creative projects.

To achieve different colors, start by familiarizing yourself with the color wheel, which illustrates primary, secondary, and tertiary colors. Begin by blending equal parts of two primary colors to create a secondary color; for example, mixing blue and yellow yields green. Experiment with varying ratios to create different shades and tints, such as adding white to a color for a lighter tint, or incorporating black for a darker shade. Use a clean workspace and tools to avoid cross-contamination of colors, and remember to condition the clay thoroughly to ensure even mixing. Keep notes of your combinations to replicate or adjust colors in future projects, allowing for a deeper understanding of color relationships and ultimately leading to more vibrant creations.

A basic color wheel is a great first guide for anyone who's just starting to mix colors. The wheel below includes these color categories, which are also shown on separate wheels:

- **Primary colors.** Red, blue, and yellow are called primary because all other colors are mixed from them.
- **Secondary colors.** These three colors are each the mixture of two primaries: orange = red + yellow; green = yellow + blue; and violet = blue + red.
- **Tertiary colors.** These six colors are each a mixture of a primary and a secondary. Their names are hyphenated, with the first word in the name indicating which of the primary colors is dominant.

COLORWAY 1: FULL WHEEL

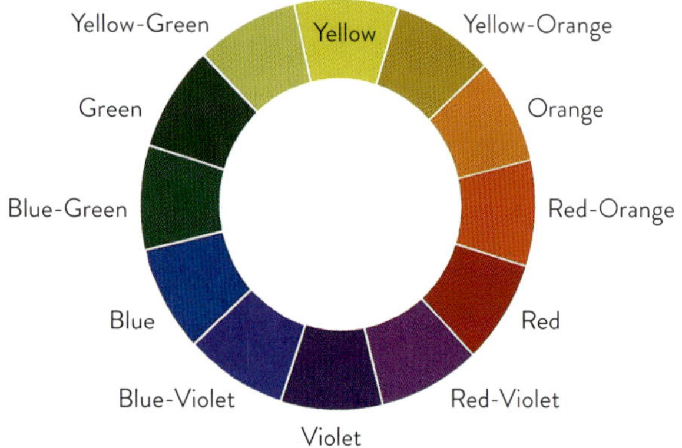

PRIMARY COLORS

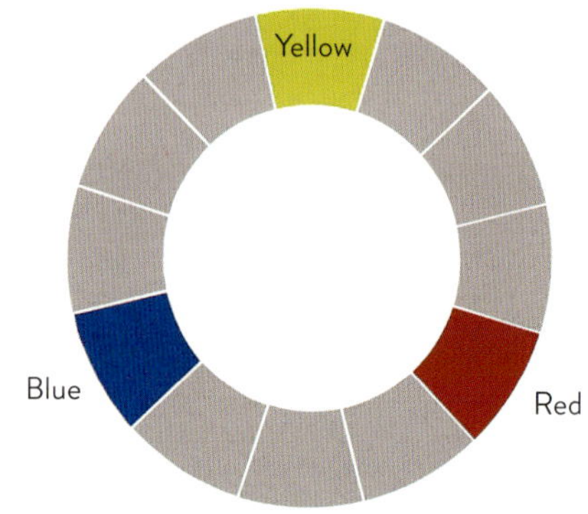

SECONDARY COLORS

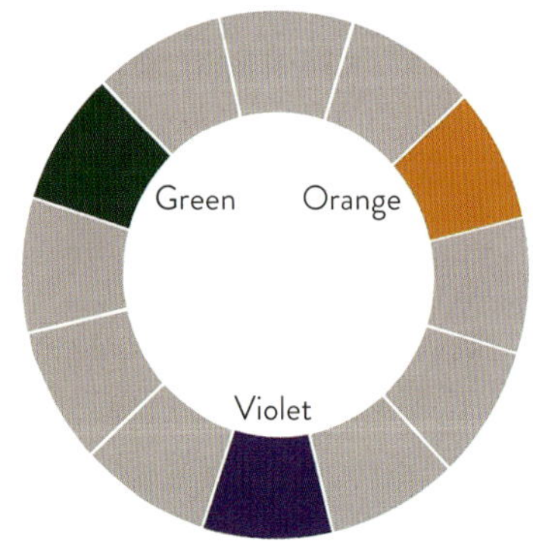

TERTIARY COLORS

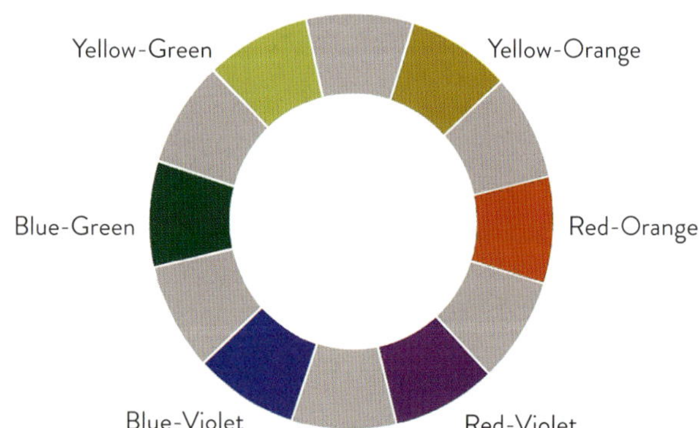

My Color Wheels

The color wheels that I use are based on modified palettes, or colorways, that feature toned, or modified, colors. I prefer working with premixed colors to using the "pure" colors of the standard wheel, which I find harsh. The colors on the wheel on the previous page are more in line with those of a traditional wheel; the colors in the wheel below are lighter and more modified.

The benefits of creating custom colors are endless. Though many polymer clay brands offer a range of premixed colors from the primaries to subtle tones, when you're able to mix and create your own unique colors, you have complete control over the outcome of your own artistic projects. By mixing custom colors, you can achieve the exact shades and tones that speak to you or the project you're starting, and allow you to truly personalize and customize your art, resulting in one-of-a-kind pieces. Moreover, custom colors can evoke specific emotions and moods, allowing you to convey your desired message through your artwork and designs.

COLORWAY 2: FULL WHEEL

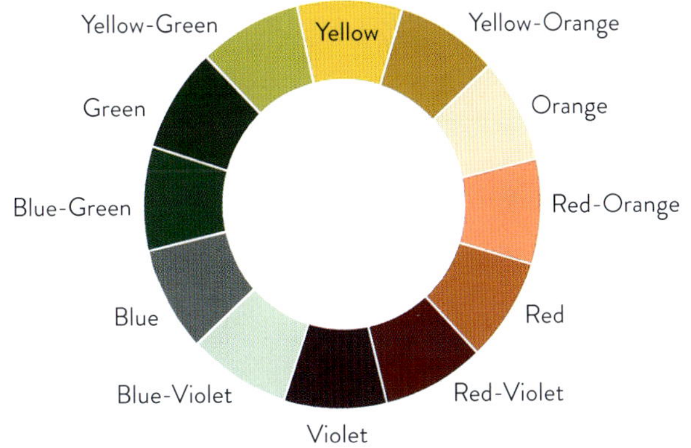

PRIMARY COLORS

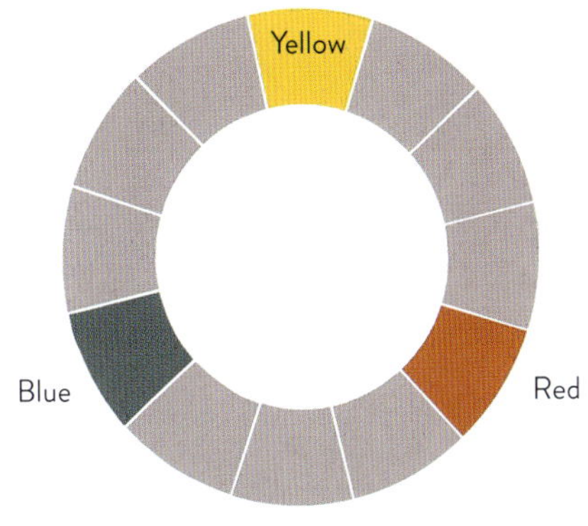

SECONDARY COLORS

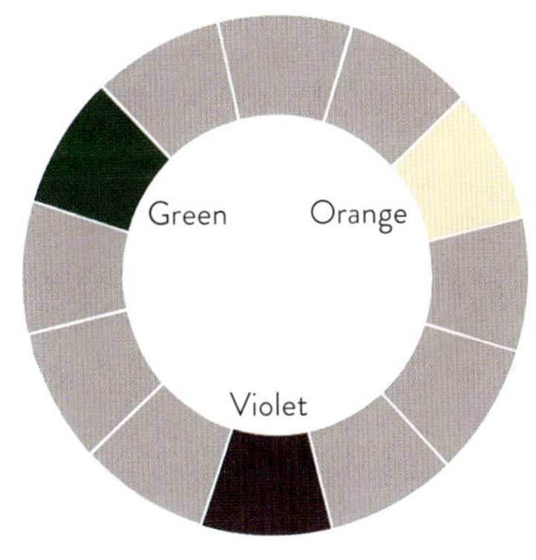

TERTIARY COLORS

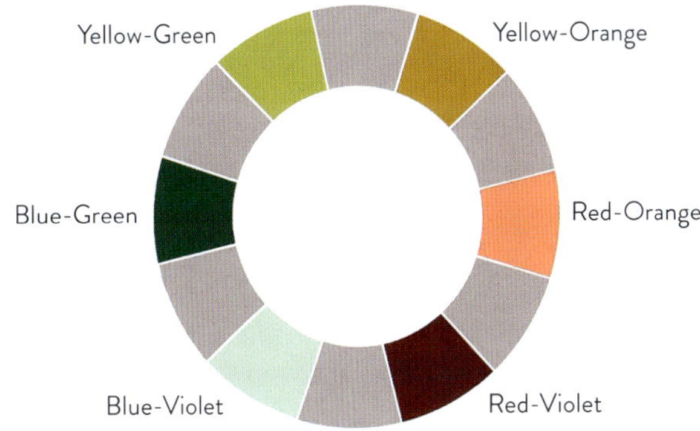

Properties of Color

The following terms are essential to an understanding of color and its characteristics.

Hue. A color in its purest form.

Shade. A color that's been mixed with black.

Tint. A color that's been mixed with white.

Tone. A color that's been mixed with gray.

Value. The lightness or darkness of a hue.

Saturation or Intensity. The brightness or dullness of a color.

Cool. Cool colors are those in which blue are dominant, including shades of blue, green, and purple.

Warm. Warm colors encompass those in which red and yellow are dominant, including orange.

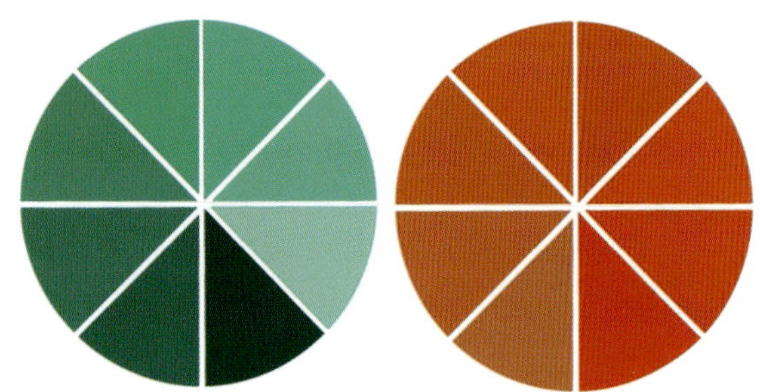

Saturation and Hue. The saturation of a hue—shown unmixed in the bottom right portion of each wheel—is lessened when it's mixed with white, gray, black, or another color.

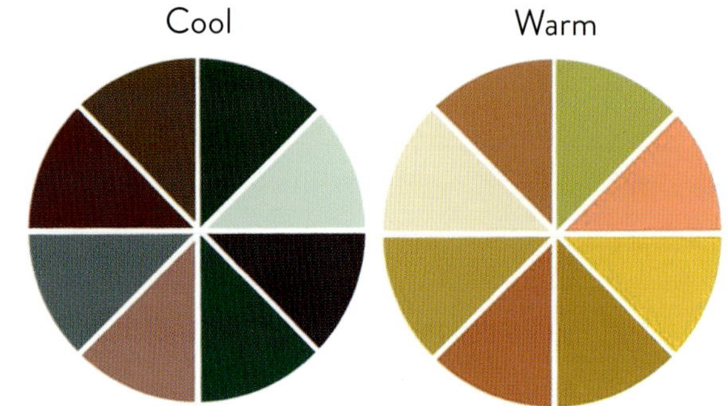

Cool and warm colors shown in wheels.

Tints (a color + white).

Shades (a color + black).

Mixing Color

The Four-Part Rule for Color Recipes

When mixing colors with polymer clay, it's important to keep in mind that the colors you're working with may not be as pure or as clear as those shown on the wheel. Start by simply playing around with color mixing. Use small amounts of clay to avoid wasting product.

One method of measuring clay in small amounts for color mixing is to roll it out and use a cutter to get the exact same shape and size per color being mixed. From there you can measure by cutting your clay into 2, 4, 8, or 16 parts, depending on the color recipe. These numbers can either be divided into or are factors of 4, which is why it's called the four-part rule.

You can use the same recipe in larger quantities; for example, one part can be one block of clay, as long as all the other parts are increased proportionally.

Color Mixing Exercise: Earth Green

WHAT YOU'LL NEED

2 parts Sculpey Soufflé in Cowboy (a dark brown), cut in 2

1 part Sculpey Soufflé in Canary (a medium yellow), cut in 4

1 part Sculpey Soufflé in Midnight Blue (a dark blue), cut in 4

Tissue blade

Acrylic roller

A

B

C

1. Start with exactly the same amount of each color (A).
2. Cut the amount you need from each color: ½ Cowboy, ¼ Canary, and ¼ Midnight Blue. You can confirm that you have the right amount of each color by putting the pieces together into the shape you started with (B).
3. Combine the pieces and mix them into your desired color (C), the same way as you would when conditioning the clay (see page 30).

Scan to see three mixes that each combine the same amount of one color with a different amount of white, black, and a second color.

I like to mix colors that reflect the colors I use to decorate my home.

Nine Color Recipes to Try

Shown opposite are some of my tried-and-true color recipes—some of the ones I use the most. This palette of colors is versatile and can provide you with a fantastic starting palette of unique colors to have on hand for the projects in this book.

When preparing these recipes, please take note that all the color names are specific to Sculpey Soufflé. And don't forget the four-part rule. Let's jump in!

Plum

¾ Tulip
⅛ Poppyseed
⅛ Cowboy

Merlot

¾ Cherry Pie
¼ Poppyseed

Toasted Cinnamon

½ Cinnamon
¼ Igloo
¼ Cowboy

Peacock

½ Jade
¼ Racing Green
⅛ Poppyseed
⅛ Midnight Blue

Velvet Chartreuse

¾ Pistachio
¼ Cowboy

Winter Sage

¾ Igloo
1/16 Cowboy
1/16 Midnight Blue
⅛ Pistachio

Golden Hour

¾ Canary
¼ Cowboy
a pinch of Pumpkin

Mojave Sunset

½ Cinnamon
¼ Igloo
⅛ Ballet
⅛ Cowboy

Natural Linen

¾ Igloo
¼ Latte

Conditioning Clay

Before using your polymer clay, it's important to take the time to condition it. This means working with it until it's soft and malleable. Sometimes, when a package of clay is first opened, it can be difficult to work with. Though this isn't always the case, it may crumble when rolled or shaped. This is why it's essential to condition the clay, because without soft clay, you're limited in what you can create.

How to Condition Clay

There are two popular ways of conditioning polymer clay: by hand or with a clay machine. With experience, you may find that depending on the dryness of the clay, you may use both methods to condition your clay.

- **Conditioning your clay by hand** is a bit more difficult. It's recommended to only condition 2 ounces (57 g) at a time. Work the clay by kneading, twisting, and squishing it, ensuring the entire piece is worked. When it has been conditioned, the clay will be soft to the touch. The warmth of your hands can speed the process, as clay naturally softens in warmer conditions.

- **Conditioning your clay with a clay machine** makes conditioning a much easier process. In this lesson, I use the Marcato Atlas 180 machine. The clay is fed through the clay machine and folded several times. After repeating this process about 15 times, the clay should be conditioned.

Tip

Look for air bubbles and try to condition them out by folding in the direction that will push the bubbles out. This will probably take a series of folds.

WHAT YOU'LL NEED

2 parts polymer clay of choice

Tissue blade

Acrylic roller

Clay machine

Scan to see a quick demo on using a tissue blade to slice clay.

1. Prep your clay by cutting a thin slice (A).

2. Roll the clay as flat as you can with your acrylic roller (B). This will require some elbow grease, but flattening it makes it much easier to roll through your machine.

Tip

If clay is cold, it'll take more time to condition. Use your hands or a pocket to warm up clay. Don't try to warm it in the oven, because exposure to higher temperatures may start to cure it.

3. Start by rolling your clay through the clay machine at the thickest setting (C), then folding it in half and rolling it through again.
4. Set it to your desired thickness. I prefer to use setting 4 for thickness with my jewelry. Continue to roll it through (D), fold it (E), and roll it through again. Do this 10 to 12 times to ensure clay is conditioned.
5. Remember to look for bubbles. What may seem like a tiny bump will bake into a bubble that may ruin your piece. If you see bubbles, fold your clay corner to corner and run it through your machine in the direction that'll push that bubble up and out. If it's being really stubborn, you can pop it with your precision knife to release the air and continue conditioning.

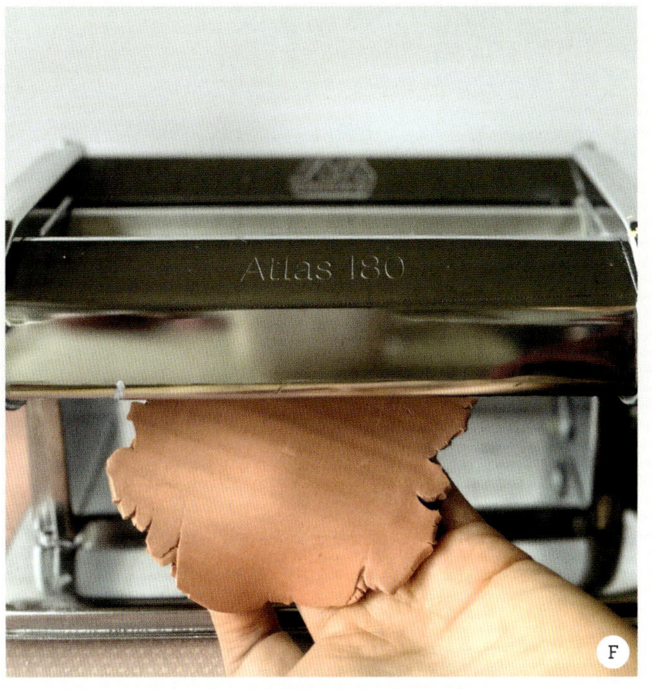

6. When finished, your clay should look smooth with a uniform thickness and no air pockets (F, G). It should be soft and malleable.

7. You'll know your clay isn't conditioned fully if it crumbles when you put it through the clay machine (H). If it looks brittle and falls apart (I), this means you need to continue conditioning.

Techniques for Beginners

In this chapter, we explore a variety of techniques that are perfect for beginners looking to delve into the art of working with polymer clay. Whether you're a novice or you have some experience with polymer clay, mastering these fundamental techniques will set a solid foundation for your clay journey. From creating textures to screen printing, each technique will be a step toward artistic freedom. So gather your tools, clear your workspace, and prepare to immerse yourself in the world of polymer clay.

Working with Texture Sheets

Used to apply intricate patterns and texture to polymer clay, silicone texture sheets are a versatile tool. These sheets are made of a flexible material that allows for the easy transfer of designs to the clay surface, making it easy for beginners and experienced crafters alike to add depth and dimension to a piece.

Another great benefit of using silicone texture sheets is their durability, as they can be reused multiple times without losing shape or detail.

We'll talk about other ways to add texture to clay pieces later in this book, but for now, let's dive in!

WHAT YOU'LL NEED

- 2 parts polymer clay (color of choice; I used my Sculpey Soufflé Mojave Sunset recipe, page 29)
- Clay machine
- Silicone texture sheet
- Acrylic roller
- Cutters
- Baking sheet and parchment paper
- Oven
- Finishing tools
- Pliers
- Jewelry findings

1. Prepare your polymer clay by conditioning it with your clay machine and rolling out a sheet to the desired thickness (A).

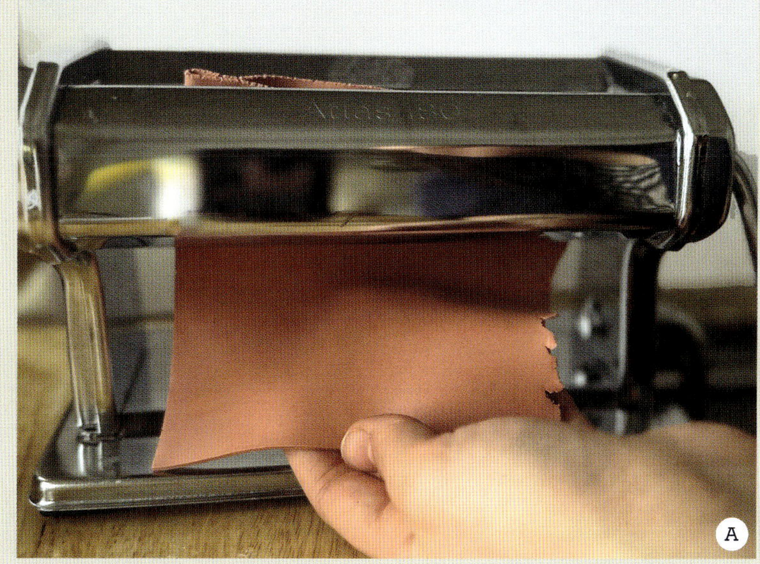

A

2. Choose a texture sheet (B).

B

C

D

E

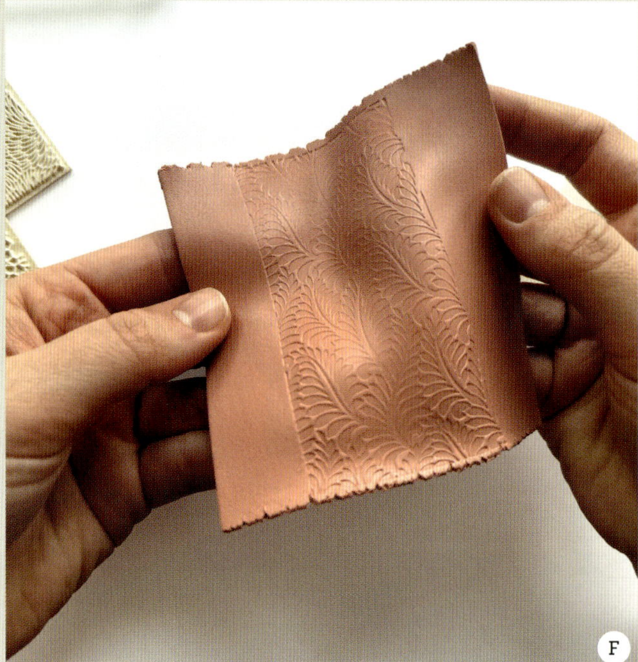
F

3. Place the sheet texture side down on the clay, then gently press the texture sheet into the clay (C).
4. Use a roller to apply even pressure across the entire sheet (D).
5. Remove the texture sheet by slowly peeling it from the top down (E, F).

G

H

I

J

6. Once you've removed the texture sheet, cut the clay into the desired shapes (G), then remove the excess (H, I).

7. Transfer the textured shapes to a baking sheet. Bake according to the clay manufacturer's directions. Sand and drill the baked shapes, then assemble your jewelry using the desired findings (J) (see Jewelry Hardware & Findings, page 22).

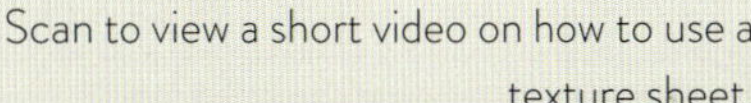
Scan to view a short video on how to use a texture sheet.

Knitted Sweater Effect

Use an extruder to create string-like clay that can be woven together to mimic a knitted sweater. This is a fun technique to explore, and it's a great way to familiarize yourself with the extruder tool, which offers many cool tricks.

WHAT YOU'LL NEED

- 2 parts polymer clay each for "yarn" twists (two colors of choice; I used my Sculpey Soufflé recipes for Peacock and Velvet Chartreuse, page 29)
- 2 parts polymer clay for base (I used my Sculpey Soufflé recipe for Peacock, page 29)
- Extruder with small circular insert
- Precision knife
- Tissue blade
- Cutters
- Baking sheet and parchment paper
- Oven
- Finishing tools
- Jewelry findings

A

B

C

1. Select and condition two colors of clay. Prepare your extruder (A).
2. Roll your clay into small logs and insert as much of one color as you can into the extruder (B).
3. The extruder comes with many size inserts. Select a small circular insert. After adding the clay to the extruder, screw on the lid, and use the handle to crank and apply pressure. This will push the clay through the hole. You should end up with a pile of string-like clay. Use your precision cutter to slice off the strings from the extruder (C). Clean out the extruder by using a finger or tool to remove all clay from the walls on the inside. Repeat the step with the second color.
4. Now that you have two piles of extruded clay, select a base color. I'm going to use the Peacock color. Make sure your base is conditioned and rolled to a uniform thickness.

5. Start by selecting a strand of one color of extruded clay and cutting it into two equal pieces using your precision knife. Twist the two pieces around one another, creating a twist (D). Create a few twists like this. Remember which way you twist the pieces, because you'll need to twist the second color in the opposite direction.

6. Starting from the left side of your slab, lay the coiled clay across from top to bottom. Apply gentle pressure to secure it to the slab of clay without denting the twists. Cut off the excess at the bottom. Keep the excess clay in good shape, because we'll continue using it.

7. Repeat step 5 with the second color, but be sure to twist the clay strands in the **opposite** direction of the first color (E). This will give the finished texture the illusion of a true knit.

8. Alternate the coiled clay colors until your slab is full (F, G, H).
9. Trim excess clay twists from the top with your tissue blade (I) to create an even slab (J).
10. Select your cutters and cut your slab into the desired shapes (K).
11. Remove the excess clay. Bake according to the clay manufacturer's directions.
12. Sand, drill, and assemble your pieces (see page 112).

Scan to see a quick video showing the process for creating this effect.

Silk Screens

The use of silk screens can be a simple way to make your pieces stand out. With a large selection of patterns and designs, silk screens are easily accessible, making them a limitless option for beginners who want to introduce a different look to their art.

WHAT YOU'LL NEED

- 2 parts polymer clay (I used my Sculpey Soufflé recipe for Plum, page 29)
- Silk screen
- Acrylic paint of choice
- Flat, rigid item, such as an old credit card or a piece of cardstock
- Cutter
- Baking sheet and parchment paper
- Oven
- Finishing tools

1. Prepare your polymer clay by conditioning it with your clay machine and rolling it out to your desired thickness (A).
2. Lay the silk screen face down onto the clay.
3. Apply a line of paint across the silk screen at the top of the clay (B).

4. Using a flat card, spread the paint across the entire silk screen sheet and clay (C). Pay close attention to spots that may need more paint.
5. Apply more paint if needed and spread again (D).
6. Once your silk screen is fully covered, peel it off from one side to the other (E).
7. Allow the paint to dry fully before cutting into the clay (F). This may take 1 hour.

G

Tip

Rinse the silk screen under warm water after use to wash off all excess paint; lay flat to dry.

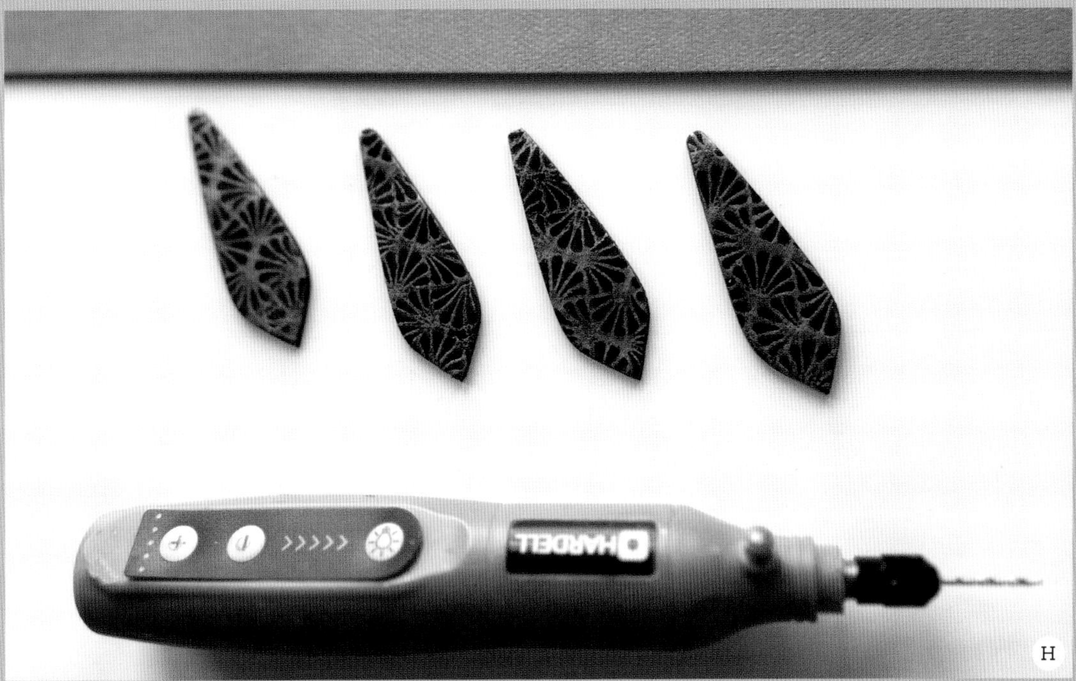

H

8. Choose a cutter shape and cut out clay pieces, removing any excess (G).
9. Bake according to the clay manufacturer's directions.
10. Sand, drill, and assemble your pieces (H) (see pages 112 and 118).

Two-Toned Texture

Using your silicone texture sheets, you can accomplish an entirely new look, that's different from the texture sheet tutorial on page 36. This is a great way to add layering to your clay and create depth.

This technique can be a bit more challenging than the others in this chapter. For beginners, I recommend trying this technique for the first time using two very similar colors. That way, you can mix it all back into one color and not waste clay.

WHAT YOU'LL NEED

2 parts polymer clay for main color (I used Sculpey Soufflé in Igloo)

1 part polymer clay for secondary color (I used Sculpey Soufflé in Mojave Sunset, see page 29)

Clay machine

Silicone texture sheet

Tissue blade

Acrylic roller

Cutters

Baking sheet and parchment paper

Oven

Finishing tools

1. Prepare your polymer clay by conditioning it with your clay machine and rolling it out to your desired thickness.
2. Select a texture sheet and a secondary clay color.

Tip The softer the clay, the easier it is to accomplish this look.

3. Prepare your secondary clay color. It should be softened and conditioned well. Using the pressure of your thumb, press the clay into the texture sheet (A), ensuring every nook is filled with clay (B). This part can be tricky. Don't put clay on top of already pressed clay, or it'll stick to itself and pull out from the design.

A

B

C

D

4. Using your tissue blade, trim off the excess clay, moving in the direction of the design (C). You'll reveal the indented design filled with clay (D). See the tip at right for handling the texture sheet.
5. Once your texture sheet is fully trimmed and the only clay on it is what is in the nooks of the design, lay it face down on the conditioned slab of primary-colored clay.
6. Use your hands to ensure the sheet is secure by pushing it into the clay slab. Use your acrylic roller to apply a lot of pressure and evenly roll over the texture sheet. Do this a few times to ensure the clay from the slab and the clay in the texture sheet have made contact.

Stabilize the Texture Sheet

Don't let the silicone texture sheet move, or it may affect the outcome of your slab (E).

E

F

G

H

7. Very slowly pull back your texture sheet, working from bottom to top (E).
8. With luck, you have successfully transferred the secondary-color design on top of your clay slab (F). This may take a few attempts, as it can be difficult to get a complete transfer on your first try.
9. Cut your clay into desired shapes and remove excess clay (G).
10. Transfer to your baking sheet and bake according to the manufacturer's directions.
11. Sand, drill, and assemble your pieces (H) (see pages 112 and 118).

Creating Stone Effects

In this chapter we dive into one of my favorite techniques. Polymer clay feels like magic, as it has the power to create stones that look incredibly real—that is, if you use the correct methods and tools. Together, we start at the basics of creating stones, and then use those basic techniques to dive further into the realism of it. When using the right materials, the outcome can be unbelievable.

Simple Crystals & Stones

This is the basic technique you'll need to not only create magical crystals and stones, but also to take it to the next level and create lookalike stones that could almost pass for the real things. This technique can be used with any colors, with or without translucent clay. You can also add things like gold leaf into the chopped mix to add hints of gold throughout your stone. There are so many ways to make this technique uniquely yours.

WHAT YOU'LL NEED

2 parts translucent polymer clay (I used Sculpey Premo)

Clay machine

Dime size (18 mm dia.) each polymer clay (three colors of choice; I used my recipes for Sculpey Soufflé in Peacock, Plum, and Golden Hour, page 29) or alcohol ink

Tissue blade

White acrylic paint of choice

Disposable gloves

Translucent liquid polymer clay (I used Liquid Sculpey)

1 piece gold leaf

Acrylic roller or acrylic sheets for shaping

Cutters

Baking sheet and parchment paper

Oven

Resin (optional)

Finishing tools

Jewelry findings

A

B

1. Condition your translucent clay (A). Select the colors you want to mix in to create your crystal or stone. Here I'm using colors from the recipes on page 29 for Peacock, Plum, and Golden Hour. You can also use alcohol ink or polymer clay to add colors to the translucent clay.
2. Take a small amount, maybe thumbnail size or less, of your color and add it to your translucent clay. Thoroughly mix the clay together using your clay machine. The amount of clay you add will change the vibe of the stone. Have fun with this—no matter what, the outcome will be beautiful (B).
3. Once the colored clay is mixed and conditioned, dice it up into bits of equal size (C). I like to add some bits of plain translucent clay for a little more depth and variety.

C

D

Tips

Using white or black acrylic paint tends to create the most unique veins.

To prevent clay and paint from sticking to your acrylic roller, lay a piece of parchment paper over the slab before rolling it.

E

F

4. Mix the piles of clay together and add an acrylic paint color of choice (D). Be sure to start with less paint and add more as needed. You want your pieces to be coated, not drenched.
5. Mix your clay pieces together until fully coated.
6. At this point, you can add some gold leaf into your clay to add more depth. Add one piece and mix thoroughly (E). Drizzle translucent Liquid Sculpey across the top of your mixed clay pile, then thoroughly mix that as well (F).

G

H

I

J

7. Using your hands, form the clay pieces into a dense log. You can then use your roller or acrylic sheets to press firmly on each side to create a squared-off log (G).

8. Use your tissue blade to slice your log into even pieces (H). Be sure not to slice it too thin (no smaller than ¼-inch).

9. Lay your clay pieces next to one another to form a slab (I). Fill in any gaps with excess pieces, and then use your acrylic roller to roll and apply even pressure across the slab (J).

10. Once the slab's surface is smooth and even (K), cut out your clay into desired shapes, removing any excess (L). Bake according to the clay manufacturer's directions.

11. If desired, add a coat of resin (see page 114) to the top of the earrings to create a dome effect (M). This will give a beautiful and professional finish to your pieces. Sand, drill, and assemble your pieces (see pages 112 and 118) (N).

Royston Ribbon Turquoise

This stone is uniquely beautiful and stands out. Discovering the process of creating it with polymer clay was a series of trials and errors. I'm so excited to share the technique I came up with to create this amazing stone.

WHAT YOU'LL NEED

4 parts (1 block) translucent polymer clay (I used Cernit)

Tissue blade

2 parts white translucent polymer clay (I used Sculpey Igloo)

White acrylic paint

Clay machine

Acrylic roller

Disposable gloves

Dark brown acrylic paint of choice

Paintbrush

½ part Turquoise polymer clay (see recipe below)

Cutters

Baking sheet and parchment paper

Oven

Resin (optional)

Finishing tools

Jewelry findings

Turquoise Recipe

Mix the Turquoise used in this tutorial by combining the following Sculpey Soufflé colors:

2 parts Pistachio
1 part Midnight Blue
1 part Igloo
½ part Cowboy

A

B

1. Divide a full block of Cernit translucent into 4 pieces.
2. Add a bit of white clay to 3 of the 4 translucent clay pieces (A). Mix it together, but not entirely. Leave a streak of white in the clay.
3. Roll your translucent and white mixture, creating a tubelike form (B). Fold and twist the tube, and then form it into a block.

C D E F

4. Dice up the block of translucent and white into bits using your tissue blade (C).
5. Also dice the remaining ¼ of the translucent clay block.
6. Mix all the diced clay together. Add some white paint and mix thoroughly. Don't drench the clay in paint (D).
7. Form the mixture into a dense log.
8. Cut the log into dime-sized pieces. Use a paintbrush to add a little bit of brown paint onto all of the sides (E).
9. Form the pieces back into a log and set aside. If you need help with these last few steps, please see the Simple Crystals & Stones tutorial on page 54.
10. Slice off 1 part of your block of white translucent polymer clay (F). Thoroughly mix a quarter-sized piece of turquoise clay with it using your clay machine.

G

H

I

J

11. Chop your clay mixture into small pieces.
12. Coat each piece with dark brown acrylic paint (G, H). Get creative with the turquoise if you want to create a multi-toned turquoise stone. Consider adding more brown to some pieces, or maybe more turquoise.
13. Form into a log and set aside.
14. Cut the block of clay you set aside in Step 9 directly down the middle (I).
15. Use the dark brown paint and a finger or paintbrush to coat the exposed sides of your cut log with paint (J).
16. Using your turquoise log from Step 13 and the acrylic roller, adjust the slice of the log of turquoise to fit in between the two sliced pieces like a sandwich (K). You want the turquoise center to be thin (no smaller than ¼-inch [6.4 mm]), so cut off any excess clay.

K
L
M
N

17. Using your acrylic roller, roll each side of the newly formed log to ensure everything is formed together.

18. Once your log feels secure, use your tissue blade to slice the log (L). With this technique, I like to slice and roll out each piece, one at a time (M). This is because the ribbon of turquoise is supposed to go directly down the middle of each piece.

19. When your piece is rolled out, use a cutter to cut it to your desired shape (N).

20. Repeat Steps 18 and 19 until you have used up your clay log. Bake according to the clay manufacturer's directions.

21. If you'd like to add a coat of resin to the top of the earrings to create a dome effect, you can (see page 114). This will give a beautiful and professional finish to your pieces.

22. Sand, drill, and assemble your pieces (see pages 112 and 118).

Rainbow Moonstone

Rainbow moonstone is a beautiful stone known for its flash of color and sparkle in different lights. In this tutorial, we learn how to recreate that unique signature flash with polymer clay and metallic paint.

WHAT YOU'LL NEED

Tissue blade

1 block (4 parts) translucent polymer clay (I used Cernit)

½ part white pearlescent polymer clay (I used Sculpey Premo Pearl)

Very pale blue acrylic paint (I used Lumiere by Jacquard 576 Hi-Lite Blue)

Liquid translucent polymer clay (I used Liquid Sculpey)

Acrylic roller or acrylic sheets for shaping

Clay machine

Paintbrush

Disposable gloves

Cutters

Baking sheet and parchment paper

Oven

Resin

Finishing tools

Jewelry findings

A

B

1. Use a tissue blade to chop 1 block of translucent polymer clay and 1/8 block of white pearlescent polymer clay into small pieces. Be sure to chop the white pearlescent clay into much smaller pieces than the translucent (A).
2. Mix the chopped pieces of clay together (B) and add a small amount of paint, mixing thoroughly until every piece is coated (C). Note that the clay should be coated in paint, not soaked in it.

C

D

E

F

G

3. Repeat the previous step using liquid translucent polymer clay. Again, coat the clay with liquid clay rather than applying it heavily.
4. Use your hands to form the clay pieces into a dense log, then use your acrylic roller or acrylic sheets to press it firmly on each side to create a tightly packed square log (D).
5. Use the tissue blade to slice the log into even pieces (E). Be sure not to slice them too thinly.
6. Lay your clay pieces next to one another to form a slab (F). If needed, use excess pieces to fill in gaps, then use your acrylic roller to roll and apply even pressure across the slab until it becomes one smooth, even surface.
7. Roll your clay slab through your clay machine at a 2 thickness, then fold it in half and roll it through once more (G). Then roll it through one final time to your desired thickness.

Evaluating the Painted Surface

As you're painting rainbow moonstone, you should view the clay surface from multiple angles to ensure that you can see the flash of blue that characterizes this stone. It's difficult to tell how much paint you actually need if you haven't looked at it from different angles.

8. Use a paintbrush to paint the top of your slab with the paint (H). Don't coat the entire slab; instead, add organic strokes across it, leaving some spots unpainted. Also, use your finger to smudge the paint to make it look more organic and less like brushstrokes. This is crucial in achieving a realistic outcome.
9. Once the paint has dried completely, cut the clay into your desired shapes (I). Remove any excess clay.
10. Bake your pieces according to the manufacturer's instructions. Let cool. Add a coat of resin to the tops of the pieces to create a domed effect, which will give them a beautiful and professional finish (see page 114). Sand and drill as needed (J), then assemble using jewelry findings (see page 118).

Onyx

Onyx is a beautiful bold stone that is surprisingly therapeutic and easy to recreate with polymer clay.

WHAT YOU'LL NEED

1 block (4 parts) black polymer clay (I used Sculpey Soufflé in Poppyseed)

Tissue blade

White acrylic paint

Disposable gloves

Acrylic roller or acrylic sheets for shaping

Cutters

Baking sheet and parchment paper

Oven

Resin (optional)

Finishing tools

Jewelry findings

A

B

1. Dice your black clay (A) into pieces (B).

C

D

E

F

2. Sparingly add white paint (C) and mix until each piece is coated, not drenched (D). Allow the paint a few minutes to dry.
3. Using your hands, form the clay pieces into a dense log. You can then use your roller or acrylic sheets to press firmly on each side to create a secure, squared-off log (E).
4. Use your tissue blade to slice your log into even pieces (F). Don't slice the pieces too thinly (no thinner than 1/4-inch [6.4 mm]).

G

H

I

5. Lay the clay pieces next to one another to form a slab (G). Fill in any gaps with excess pieces.

6. Use your acrylic roller to roll your slab, applying even pressure until it has become a smooth, even surface (H).

7. Cut the clay into your desired shapes (I), removing any excess clay. Bake according to the clay manufacturer's directions.

8. If you'd like to add a coat of resin to the surface to create a domed effect, you can (see page 114). This will give a beautiful and professional finish to your pieces.

9. Sand, drill, and assemble your pieces (see pages 112 and 118).

Howlite

Howlite is almost the inverse of onyx, providing the same beautiful bold statement but a little softer. With a white coloring and black veins, this stone transitions though all seasons. We'll use the same technique as onyx, but with the colors reversed.

WHAT YOU'LL NEED

1 block (4 parts) white polymer clay (I used Sculpey Soufflé in Igloo)

Tissue blade

Black acrylic paint of choice or black alcohol ink

Liquid polymer clay (I used Liquid Sculpey, about enough for a "drizzle")

Disposable gloves

Acrylic roller or acrylic sheets for shaping

Cutters

Baking sheet and parchment paper

Oven

Resin (optional)

Finishing tools

Jewelry findings

A

B

1. Dice your white clay (A) into pieces (B).

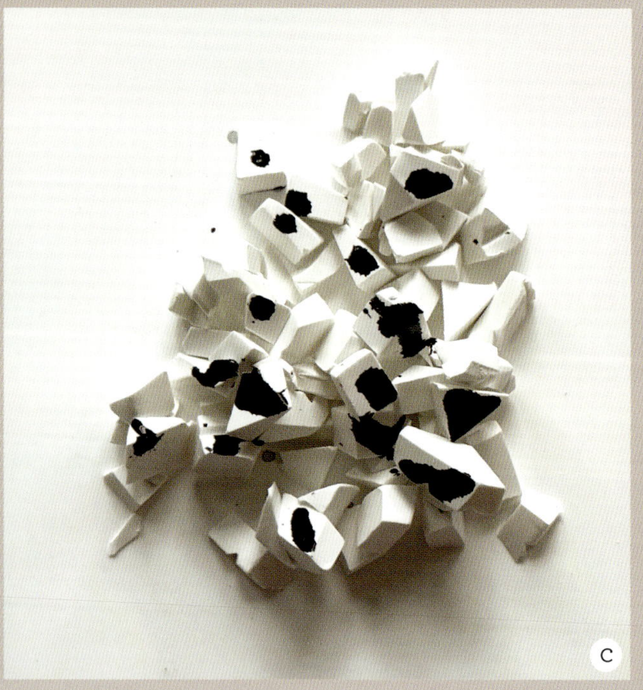

2. Add black paint or black alcohol ink (C) and mix until each piece is coated, not drenched (D). Allow the paint a few minutes to dry.

3. Using your hands, form the clay pieces into a dense log. Then use your roller or acrylic sheets to press firmly on each side to create a secure, squared-off log (E).

4. Use the tissue blade to slice your log into even pieces (F). Don't slice the pieces too thinly (no thinner than 1/4-inch [6.4 mm]).

G

H

I

5. Lay your clay pieces next to one another to form a slab (G). Fill in any gaps with excess pieces.
6. Use your acrylic roller to roll your slab, applying even pressure until it has become a smooth, even surface (H).
7. Cut the clay into your desired shapes, removing any excess clay (I). Bake according to the clay manufacturer's directions.
8. If you'd like to add a coat of resin to the top of the earrings to create a dome effect, you can (see page 114). This will give a beautiful and professional finish to your pieces.
9. Sand, drill, and assemble your pieces (see page 112 and 118).

Sliced Agate

Agate is a quartzlike stone that has a banded appearance. It's such a unique stone and can be found in many different colors. Creating agate from polymer clay takes time, but is so rewarding because the results can be amazing. I use two different brands of translucent clays: the Cernit, which cures as a tried-and-true clear, but is soft and harder to work with, and Sculpey Premo, which has a slightly yellow hue that's great for mixing with other colors.

WHAT YOU'LL NEED

2 blocks translucent polymer clay for mixing with colors (I used Sculpey Premo)

Alcohol inks or polymer clay (five or six colors of choice; I used a variety of reds, yellows, and oranges)

Clay machine

1 part translucent polymer clay for the clear center of the agate (I used Cernit)

1 package gold leaf and gold leaf separator paper

1 block translucent polymer clay for layering between colors (I used Sculpey Premo)

Tissue blade

Clay tool or paintbrush

Baking sheet and parchment paper

Oven

Resin (optional)

Jewelry findings

A

B

1. Start by mixing 2 parts of your translucent clay (I used Sculpey Premo) into the color palette that you'd like for your agate. I recommend mixing five different colors of equal parts (A). A cohesive color palette will result in a more natural-looking agate.
2. Condition those clay colors individually and roll them out into small slabs.
3. Thoroughly condition the second type of translucent clay (I used Cernit).
4. Roll your conditioned translucent clay into a small log (B).
5. Roll the translucent clay log in a piece of the gold leaf (C) until it's fully covered.

C

D

E

F

G

6. Wrap the gold-leaf log in a thin layer, about ½-inch part, of translucent clay (I used Sculpey Premo) (D). Trim any excess.

7. Take your **lightest** shade of the colored clay and roll it out on the thinnest setting your clay machine offers.

8. Cut that piece of clay to a width that matches your clay log (E). You'll apply more of this color later. Roll the log in the lightest clay color.

9. Prepare the next shade darker in the same way. Roll it out on the thinnest setting and wrap it around the log (F).

Tip

You can adjust the thickness of each layer; just be mindful not to go too thick. Two or three settings from the thinnest is okay if you want a layer to particularly pop, or you want a thicker band.

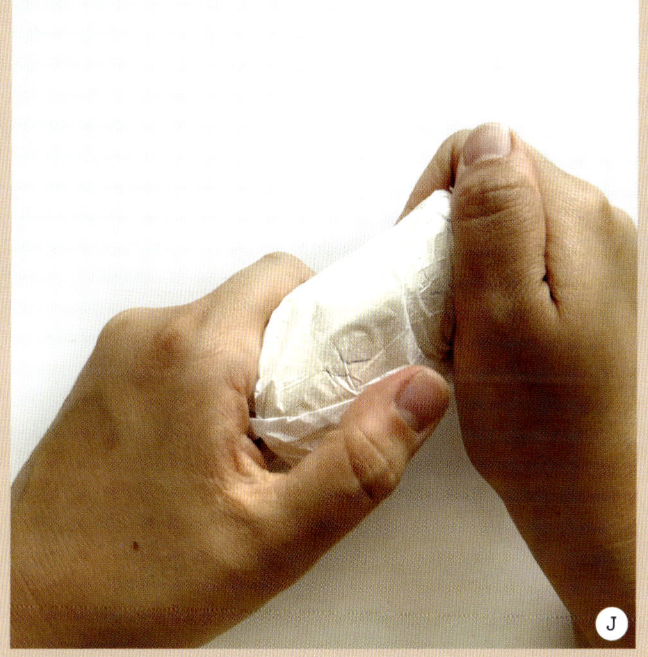

10. Repeat those two colors a few times (G) and then add a layer, about ½ part, of translucent clay (I used Sculpey Premo) to your log (H).

11. Repeat Steps 7 to 10 with the third and second darkest shades. Be mindful to periodically add the translucent clay (I used Sculpey Premo) throughout this process).

12. Repeat Steps 7 to 10 with the two darkest colors. Feel free to add pops of the lighter colors in this last step to use up your clay. Be mindful to keep this part on the darker side though.

13. Once you have finished up your colored clay, add on a final layer of the translucent clay (J). Roll the entire log in gold leaf until the gold leaf has bonded with the clay, then brush off the excess leaf.

Working with Gold Leaf

Use gold leaf separator paper to really adhere the leaf to the clay without getting the leaf stuck to your hands.

14. Roll the log to your desired thickness.
15. Using your fingers, a clay tool, or the stick of a paintbrush, try to organically squeeze the log to add natural indentations like an agate has.
16. Using your tissue blade, cut off about 1 inch (2.5 cm) of the log's end to ensure each layer is visible as you continue to make slices (K).
17. Cut the remaining log into thin slices and roll through your clay machine at a 3 setting to get a uniform thickness (L). Do one slice at a time. That way you can see how big the slices become after rolling it out, you can also adjust the direction you roll it through the machine to get different and more organic shapes.
18. Once you have sliced and rolled out all of your clay, bake it according to the clay manufacturer's instructions. If you'd like to add a coat of resin to the top of the earrings to create a dome effect, you can (see page 114). This will give a beautiful and professional finish to your pieces. This will also protect the gold leaf from tarnishing.
19. Note there is **no sanding** needed on these! Just drill and assemble (M).

Bonus Tutorial: Agate Slab

You can also combine your sliced agate pieces to create a unique agate slab.

1. Piece together the slices. Roll it out with your acrylic roller and then run the slab through your clay machine to get a uniform thickness (A).
2. Using cutters of choice, cut your shapes (B) and remove excess clay.
3. Transfer to a baking sheet. Bake according to the clay manufacturer's directions.
4. Once it has baked and cooled, add a layer of resin to give a professional finish (see page 114).
5. Sand, drill, and assemble your pieces (see pages 112 and 118) (C).

A

B

C

Gallery: Minted Mire

Julia Sprow is the artist behind Minted Mire (@mintedmire on Instagram). The juxtaposition of "minted" (fresh/new) and "mire" (mud) perfectly describes where her inspiration comes from: the world directly underneath our feet. Opals have always been her favorite stone, and she was determined to mimic this mysterious volcanic rock with polymer clay. It was quite a challenge, but worth every failed experiment to get to the final results!

Exploring Other Mediums

In this chapter, we'll touch base on some of my favorite techniques and methods that involve using more than just clay. We'll learn how to create a slab that has a galaxy captured inside, how to paint on clay, and even how to incorporate real pressed flowers. These techniques all require the use of resin as a layer of protection. Once you learn the basics, your brain will blossom with ideas.

Galaxy Effect

The galaxy unfolds in a magnificent tapestry of colors, as swirling blues, vibrant stars, and shimmering golds dance across the vastness of space. Using the right techniques, we can capture this ethereal beauty and translate it into a tactile form. By using alcohol inks with the deep hues of the cosmos, we can mold our clay into representations of celestial skies.

WHAT YOU'LL NEED

- 1 block (4 parts) translucent polymer clay (I used Sculpey Premo)
- Tissue blade
- Clay machine
- Acrylic roller
- Paper towels
- Alcohol ink variety pack (I used Piccassio in sapphire blue, sky blue, blue-green, purple, violet, green, white, and black)
- Metallic alcohol ink variety pack (I used Piccassio in metallic gold and metallic silver)
- Drinking straw
- Paintbrush
- Green pigment powder (I used Pearl Ex Powdered Pigment in Interference Green)
- Gold pigment powder (I used Pearl Ex Powdered Pigment in Brilliant Gold)
- Disposable gloves
- Cutters
- Baking sheet and parchment paper
- Oven
- Resin
- Finishing tools
- Jewelry findings

A

B

1. Condition and roll out your translucent clay to your desired thickness. Set it flat on top of a few sheets of paper towels (A). The paper towels will soak up excess ink, so you don't stain your working surface.
2. Remove the following colors from your variety ink packs: sapphire blue, sky blue, blue-green, purple, violet, green, white, black, metallic gold, and metallic silver.
3. Start with the sapphire blue. Add a few drops onto your clay (B).

Tip

If you feel your slab has gotten too dark, use white ink to brighten up some spots. I like to use it on purples and blues to create flashes of light in the slab.

4. Quickly move the ink around by blowing through the straw (C). This will prevent the ink from seeping too quickly into one spot. Add a few drops of the sky blue and the blue-green around the sapphire blue, and repeat the process with the straw.
5. Begin to incorporate the purple and violet in small bits. Move them around with the straw and blend them in with some of the blue (D). Remember the blues are your focal colors in this slab.
6. Repeat these steps until you have covered the majority of your slab with alcohol ink. Fill in any gaps with black or green—whatever seems most fitting to you and your creation.
7. Add some drops of the gold and silver sparingly across the entirety of your slab. If you feel the metallic ink is too strong, you can drop one of the nonmetallic colors inside the metallic drop to tone it down.

F

G

8. This is a very forgiving and fun technique, so go wild with it. You can continue to add layers and depth if you aren't happy with the slab yet.

9. Dip your paint brush into the green pigment powder. Tap off excess powder into the container, then tap the brush so the powder dusts the surface of the slab (E). Repeat this step with the gold powder. Repeat until you feel you've created enough stardust.

10. Now you wait. It's **so important** that you allow your ink to dry fully before you cut into the slab or try to bake it. If you bake it before it's dry, the backside of the clay will get lots of bubbles, lessening the quality of the pieces. Allow the slab to sit for about 8 to 12 hours to fully dry.

11. Once fully dry, you can cut your clay to your desired shapes (F).

Tip Note that the ink will bleed onto your cutters. The ink "dries," but will leave a residue on anything firmly applied against it, which is why we have to seal these pieces. It's best to clean the cutters according to the manufacturer's instructions when you finish.

---

12. Carefully transfer the polymer clay pieces to a baking sheet. Bake according to the clay manufacturer's directions.

13. Seal the finished pieces. To protect the alcohol ink and enhance the colors, seal the finished polymer clay piece with resin (see page 114).

14. Sand and drill your pieces. Assemble with hardware (see pages 112 and 118) (G).

Galactic Variations

You aren't limited to these colors when using this technique to create galactic clay slabs. Take some time to research different colors and tones that exist in space in our galaxy. This technique is simply a platform for you to stand on—the real fun and creativity is when you sit down and get lost in the process.

Watercolor Effect

Using alcohol ink, we'll create a watercolor clay slab with soft tones and fluidity. Alcohol inks can be very versatile with clay.

WHAT YOU'LL NEED

- 1 block (4 parts) white polymer clay (I used Sculpey Soufflé in Igloo)
- Tissue blade
- Clay machine
- Acrylic roller
- Paper towels
- Alcohol ink variety pack (I used Piccassio in blue-green, sunset, marigold, coffee, and white)
- Drinking straw
- Cutters
- Baking sheet and parchment paper
- Oven
- Resin
- Finishing tools
- Jewelry findings

A

1. Condition and roll out your white clay to your desired thickness. Set it flat on top of a few layers of paper towels. The paper towels will soak up excess ink, so you don't stain your working surface.
2. Remove your colors of choice from the alcohol variety pack. In this tutorial, I use blue-green, sunset, marigold, coffee, and white (A).
3. Start by adding droplets of color onto the clay. I'm going to begin with blue-green. (B).

B

4. Using your straw, blow the ink around so it doesn't seep into only one spot on the clay. Continue this process with all your colors (C) until the slab is fully covered (D).

Tip Be mindful of the colors you're choosing, as some colors mix and form a muddy color.

---

5. Once your slab is fully covered, add droplets of white on top (E), using as much or as little as you like. Adding a lot causes the colors to lighten and gives the clay a cloudy watercolor look.

6. Repeat these steps as many times as you want until you've reached a slab you're happy with (F).

G

H

I

J

7. Now you wait. It's **so important** that you allow your ink to dry fully before you cut into the slab or try to bake it. If you bake it before it's dry, the backside of the clay will get lots of bubbles, lessening the quality of the pieces. Allow the slab to sit for about 8 to 12 hours to fully dry.

8. Cut out your clay to your desired shapes (G, H), removing any excess (I). Bake according to the clay manufacturer's directions.

9. To protect the ink, add a coat of resin to the top of the earrings; this will also create a domed effect (see page 114). This will give a beautiful and professional finish to your pieces.

10. Sand, drill, and assemble your pieces (J) (see pages 112 and 118).

Painting on Clay

Unleash your creativity with unique polymer clay earrings featuring hand-painted designs. Because each pair is a masterpiece of artistic expression, showcasing the freedom of paint on a miniature canvas, the tutorial shows how we created one pair of earrings—but yours will be beautifully unique. Using high-quality acrylic paint, carefully craft each earring to be one of a kind. To preserve the intricate designs and vibrant colors, seal each piece with resin, ensuring that your wearable art stays beautifully preserved for years to come. Embrace your individuality and make a statement with painted polymer clay earrings.

Tutorial by Mikayla Trapasso-Wallace

Mikayla Trapasso-Wallace is the painter behind my MAK X MINI hand-painted collaborations. She'll be guiding us through this tutorial on learning how to paint on polymer clay and create one-of-a-kind masterpieces. For more about Mikayla and to see other examples of her work, see page 100.

WHAT YOU'LL NEED

- Conditioned polymer clay
- Cutters
- Baking sheet and parchment paper
- Oven
- Paintbrushes
- Paint palette
- Water cup
- Paper towels
- Finishing marker variety pack (I used Micron 005)
- Acrylic paint of choice for primer
- Acrylic paint of choice for ombré
- Acrylic paints for subject of choice
- Hair dryer or heat gun (optional)
- Resin

A

1. Prepare your conditioned polymer clay by cutting out your desired shape. Bake according to the clay manufacturer's directions.
2. When your clay has baked and cooled, set up your painting station. You'll need your acrylic paint, brushes, a paint palette, a water cup, paper towels, and finishing markers.

Tip Micron 005 pens are my personal favorite to work with and last the longest.

3. Now that your station is ready, you can begin by priming your blank clay with a coat of white acrylic paint or your desired base color. This makes the paint stick better. I mixed a custom coral color for the base. Paint one layer and allow to dry (A), then repeat (B).

Tip Having a hair dryer or heat gun on hand will speed up the drying process in between each step.

B

4. The next step is to add a lighter tone to the center of the earring base and shade out to create an ombré effect. Start by painting a smaller oval in the center then clean your brush completely. Dip the brush into the water and gently paint around the edges for a light fade. Once you have an even ombré, let dry (C).

5. Once your base or background is set you can begin with your detailing. In this case, I'm working toward a floral bouquet. Begin with a fine-tip brush and add various green-toned leaves or greenery (D, E). Let dry completely.

Tip Princeton Velvetouch liners are great for this stage.

F

G

H

6. Starting from the outermost edge and working in, add flowers of your choosing. I'm starting with pale yellow daisies in this example. I make 6 to 8 dots in a small circle and drag each dot into the center of the flowers (F). Once that has dried, add a dot in a contrasting color to complete the center of the daisy.
7. Repeat steps with various colored flowers and continue to layer until your bouquet is filled in.
8. Once your painting is complete set aside to dry completely. This step requires a fully dry base.
9. Lastly, take your fine-tip finishing markers and carefully draw an outline on top of your base painting (G). You can make this as detailed as you would like.
10. When your work has fully dried, add a top coat of resin to preserve the art.
11. When the resin is fully cured, sand, drill, and assemble your pieces (H) (see pages 112 and 118).

Gallery: Mikayla Trapasso-Wallace

The work shown on these two pages is by Mikayla Trapasso-Wallace. A beautiful woman and my sister-in-law, Mikayla is a talented artist with a passion for painting and tattoo art. She is grounded and down-to-earth, and also excels in creating ceramic art, a skill she honed during her college studies. Inspired by nature, family, dance, and loving expressions, Mikayla's work embodies a unique blend of creativity and heartfelt inspiration.

Gallery: Olive Alchemy

Marlie is the dreamer, designer, and hand sculptor behind Olive Alchemy (@olivealchemy on Instagram). Marlie is a mixed media artist located near the heart of America. With an emphasis on folklore and mythology, she describes her jewelry as being for lovers of the enchanted and vintage. Marlie is highly skilled in sculptural work and has mastered the art of realistic flowers. Marlie has incorporated other mediums, including paint, into her clay work. In the examples shown here, Marlie has used paint to add depth and enhance detail.

Marlie is incredibly talented and her work tells a very lovely story; you can feel her soul radiate from her work. It's really an honor to call her a friend.

Pressed Flowers

Combining pressed flowers and clay is one of my favorite ways to create jewelry. It's such a whimsical blend of nature and art. The pressed flowers offer unique and vibrant colors and the finished product is always beautiful.

WHAT YOU'LL NEED

1 part each polymer clay of choice (three colors; I used Sculpey Soufflé in Cinnamon, my recipe for Mojave Sunset [page 29], and a mixture of my recipes for Peacock and Velvet Chartreuse [page 29])

Tissue blade

Clay machine

Acrylic rollers

Cutters

Pressed flowers of choice (I used yellow daisies, white daises, and Queen Anne's lace)

Cyanoacrylate glue (I used Gorilla Glue Superglue)

Tweezers

Precision knife

Resin

A

1. Prepare your polymer clay by conditioning it with your clay machine and rolling it out to your desired thickness (A).

B

2. Cut your clay to your desired shapes, removing any excess clay (B). Bake according to the clay manufacturer's directions.

Tip Make sure you select a shape that will be large enough to fit the entire flower.

3. While your clay is baking, choose and set aside the pressed flowers you'll be using to make your pieces.
4. Remove your clay from the oven and allow the pieces to fully cool.
5. Put a dot of superglue on each clay piece and spread it around with the bottle tip (C).
6. Using your fingers or tweezers, pick up your flowers and carefully set them in the glue (D, E).

C

Tip Make sure all petals are glued down. If they aren't, the petals can trap air underneath while applying resin, or the resin can cure with the petals poking out.

D

Scan to see a video on how much glue to use for this technique.

E

F

G

H

7. Allow the glue to fully dry. This should only take about 10 minutes.
8. Be sure to cut off any excess petals that go over the edge of the clay pieces (F).
9. Apply a domed coat of resin over each piece (see page 114).
10. Allow resin to cure for 48 to 72 hours.
11. Sand, drill, and assemble your pieces (G, H) (see pages 112 and 118).

Curing & Finishing Your Pieces

Baking polymer clay pieces is an essential step in the crafting process that transforms raw clay into durable and beautifully finished pieces. This doesn't require special equipment or a kiln. It can be done in something as accessible as a tabletop oven or a kitchen oven. You don't even need a separate oven, as long as you don't burn your clay.

Understanding the Baking Process

The baking process, also known as curing, involves heating the clay in an oven to a specific temperature and duration to harden and set the material. This step is crucial for ensuring that your pieces maintain their shape and durability.

Allowing your oven to fully preheat is necessary to ensure you don't disturb the curing process of your artwork. The temperature of the oven spikes as it's preheating; if your clay pieces are put in too soon, it's likely they'll burn and bubble. This isn't only devastating because you will have lost your hard work and time, but it's also not good to breathe the toxic fumes from burnt polymer clay. You can prevent burning your clay by ensuring the temperature is correct. Using a thermometer in your oven is a great method to monitor temperature.

Different brands and types of polymer clay have specific baking instructions. It's essential to follow the manufacturer's instructions to ensure your pieces cure properly. Clay that is cured correctly will be durable and flexible, while clay that hasn't been properly cured can become very brittle and may break easily. Again, this isn't something you want to happen to your art, so be mindful.

Preparing Your Pieces for Baking

After cutting out your clay shapes, you must transfer them to a baking sheet. Any flat baking pan, such as a baking sheet, will work. A ceramic tile will work as well. Something I have learned over the years is that lining your baking sheet with parchment paper or card stock first will give the backs of your clay pieces a matte and soft finish. If baked directly on a baking sheet, the clay can get spots of different sheens that look unprofessional.

Sanding & Drilling

Sanding the polymer clay edges is essential for achieving a smooth, comfortable, professional-looking finish on your jewelry pieces. After using your cutter, it's likely there will be bumps or excess clay stuck to the edges of your pieces. Sanding not only enhances the appearance and durability of your jewelry but also adds a final touch of quality and craftsmanship to your creations.

Be mindful when sanding because the polymer clay releases a dust that isn't the best to breathe in. I wear my respirator when sanding, but any sort of mask will do. Keeping your body protected inside and out is the first priority.

Essential Sanding Supplies

If you're only planning on making polymer clay pieces occasionally, sandpaper will work. You can sand your edges to remove excess clay and work your way up to a finer grit until the edges are smooth.

I personally recommend investing in a Dremel or rotary tool. I use my Dremel to sand or drill every single piece of clay I bake. A low speed and felt attachment can quickly sand clay edges smooth to the touch. Don't worry about sanding the fronts or backs unless necessary.

The Sanding Process

1. Hold the Dremel tool with your selected sanding attachment at a slight angle to the edge of the polymer clay piece.
2. Gently move the Dremel back and forth along the edges and smooth out any rough or uneven areas. Avoid applying too much pressure to prevent damage to the clay.
3. Periodically stop and check the progress of the sanding to ensure that the edges are smoothed evenly.

Drilling

Once I'm finished sanding, I rotate out my Dremel attachment for the smallest drill bit available. You can either mark the drill hole on the pieces with a pencil to ensure uniformity, or you can wing it like I do. When drilling multiple holes for attachments, I do mark, but for one single hole, I don't. I use a wooden cutting board as a base for drilling so I don't damage my working surface. A cutting board is also a stable base for drilling.

When you're ready to drill, secure the piece with one hand to prevent it from moving while drilling. With the rotary tool on high speed, hold the drill bit perpendicular to the surface of the polymer clay and drill through.

Rinsing

It's likely you now have a dusty mess. I like to give my clay pieces a bath when I'm finished with sanding and drilling. Using a glass bowl and warm water, let your pieces soak while you clean up the dust. Rinse them off and let them dry fully before assembling.

Resin Crash Course

I personally love to use resin on my pieces both for the domed glossy look and also for preservation aspects. Using resin is how I keep pressed flowers intact in my jewelry as well as handpainted pieces and alcohol ink pieces. There are two types of resin that are suitable for jewelry making.

UV Resin

UV resin is a type of resin that cures and hardens when exposed to ultraviolet (UV) light. It's a popular choice for crafting and jewelry-making due to its fast curing time and clarity. You can find a lot of UV resin options online or in craft stores. The brand I use is called OBSANG Crystal Clear Hard UV Resin.

Pros

- Cures quickly and clear with UV light
- Comes ready to use; no mixing involved
- Cures very hard

Cons

- Yellows over time
- When cured too quickly, it causes the cured polymer clay to warp in shape and not lay flat
- UV lights are small, so you can only work in small batches
- Goes on very thick

How to Apply UV Resin

1. Place your baked and cooled clay pieces on a silicone mat and add a workable amount of resin to the center of your piece.
2. Using silicone tools, spread your resin out to the edges until the entire piece is covered. Make sure it doesn't drip over the edges.
3. Using a lighter, quickly apply heat to your pieces to pop bubbles in the resin.
4. Set a UV lamp over the uncured resin pieces and allow to cure until hard, typically 1 to 2 minutes.

Two-Part Epoxy Art Resin

Two-part epoxy is a type of art resin that typically has a 24- to 72-hour cure time. It hardens as it cures and, if mixed properly, will result in rock-hard, scratch-free resin. Professional artists like using this type of resin for its versatility and durability. Quality varies from brand to brand, but it can be crystal clear and bubble-free if done right. There are many art resin brands out there and I have tried several of them. My two favorite brands are Unicone Art and Superclear Epoxy. These products reliably cure very hard, have little to no bubbles, and are crystal clear.

Pros

- Very clear, strong, and glossy
- Self-leveling
- Workable in large batches
- Longer work time
- Higher viscosity to remove bubbles

Cons

- Comes in two parts and needs to be thoroughly mixed
- Can have an odor
- Can be more expensive
- Temperature can affect the results

How to Apply Two-Part Art Resin

1. Make sure your workspace is clean and the room has a temperature of 68°F to 72°F (20°C to 22°C).
2. Determine how much resin you'll need. Using a cup with ounce or ml markings, mix your resin in two equal parts with a 1:1 ratio.
3. Using a popsicle stick, slowly mix your resin for a minimum of 4 minutes, making sure to scrape the bottom and sides of the cup (A). As you begin mixing, you'll notice steaks beginning to form. Mix your resin until there are no more streaks.
4. Let the mixed epoxy rest for a few minutes to allow bubbles to rise to the surface. Pop any bubbles with the heat from a lighter or a torch.
5. Arrange your baked and cooled clay pieces on a silicone mat.
6. Using your popsicle stick, scoop up a little bit of resin and put it in the middle of your clay piece.
7. Spread the resin out to the edges of the clay, but be sure not to go over the edge. Ensure the entire clay piece is covered in resin (B). Add a small amount more if necessary.
8. Let rest for a few minutes and hit with a torch or lighter to remove bubbles (C).
9. When you have applied resin to all of your pieces, put a cover over everything to keep fumes in and dust out.
10. Allow the pieces to sit for 24 to 72 hours before sanding the edges or drilling your pieces.

A

B

C

Assembly Basics

When you get to this point, that means you have made it to the end of your creation process, and now it's time to piece it all together.

Using pliers and jump rings, connect the pieces, ensuring that each jump ring is tightly closed. If your clay pieces are rubbing against each other or you can't properly close a jump ring, you need to go up a size in the jump ring.

Attaching Backs

If you aren't using an ear wire on your earrings, you likely need to attach a post stud to your clay pieces. There are many methods of attaching backs to polymer clay. After many trials, this is my super secure way of attaching post studs with the security of knowing they won't pop off.

Resin Attaching Method

1. Lay your piece face down (A).
2. Add a small dot of cyanoacrylate glue to the spot where you'll be attaching the stud (B, C).
3. Set the stud in the glue and push down to ensure it is secure.
4. Let the glue dry fully. This takes 10 to 12 minutes.
5. Apply a small amount of UV resin over the flat part of the stud that is glued to the clay (D).
6. Spread the resin out with a disposable or silicone tool to ensure the entire stud is covered.
7. Put the earring under the UV light and let it cure for 1 to 2 minutes.

Scan to see a quick tutorial on how to attach a fish hook ear wire.

A

B

C

D

Contributing Artists

boldrady - Betty Kuttelwascher

Brenzaart - Brenna Riley

Cutterlydesigns - Diana Andrade

makmade_ - Mikayla Trapasso-Wallace

Mintedmire - Julia Sprow

Olivealchemy - Marlie Kniss

Top left: Mintedmire - Julia Sprow

Top right: Olivealchemy - Marlie Kniss

Bottom left and right: Collaboration of Lauren Wallace and makmade_ - Mikayla Trapasso-Wallace, MAK x MINI

Resources

Brenzaart-Brenna Riley (for graphics)

cooltools.us (for many tools, silk screens, texture mats, and more)

Michaels.com (for basic tools like exacto, acrylic roller, etc)

Roclayco.com (for silicone texture mats & silk screens)

Sculpey.com (for clay)

Wholesalejewelrysupply.com (for hardware)

Acknowledgments

I want to extend a heartfelt thank you to my wonderful mother, Marian, and my supportive father, Jeff. Your belief in me throughout my unconventional life journey has been a guiding light. The invaluable gifts of art, song, and a business mind you've instilled in me are a truly dynamite combination that has shaped who I am today. Most importantly, your teachings about kindness, goodness, and maintaining a gracious heart resonate deeply within me.

To my amazing siblings, both here with me and in heaven—Kellye, Jeff, and Joey—thank you so much for always lifting me up and encouraging me in my work and artistic pursuits. Your unwavering support truly means the world to me and continues to inspire me every single day. Jeff (Richard), you are so deeply missed and longed for, but oh my, the way you enthusiastically cheered me on was irreplaceable. I will take that precious encouragement with me and carry it in my heart and mind forever.

To my soon-to-be husband, Taylor, and our beautiful daughter, Josephine, you both are my greatest motivation and inspiration. You are the reasons I push myself hard every day and fight fiercely for my goals and dreams without hesitation. Josephine, my wish for you is to experience true freedom and joy in this life, allowing you to explore all that the world has to offer. I strive daily to be the best example I can be for you, always hoping to guide you in the right direction. Thank you for joining us here on this journey and for teaching me more about life than I ever imagined I would learn.

To my incredible friends—Heather, Mackenzie, Lexie—and others, thank you for being my biggest cheerleaders since the very beginning. I couldn't have accomplished so much without each of you lifting my spirits in moments of doubt.

Lastly, to my amazing Instagram community—a vibrant collection of artists, dreamers, doers, leaders, supporters, healers, and makers—your presence in my life has been invaluable. I could not have achieved any of this without you. You have rallied behind MAED BY MINI through both the beautiful triumphs and the challenging moments, and for that, I am eternally grateful from the bottom of my heart.

About the Author

Lauren Wallace, an artist, young mother, musician, and jewelry maker, discovered her passion for crafting with polymer clay in 2019. In 2020, she took a leap of faith and started her own polymer clay jewelry business. Lauren's love for art traces back to her upbringing in a music-centered household. Her journey to pursue art as a career began after a transformative year as an exchange student in India, where she studied the intricate art of Mehndi.

Inspired by flowers, nature, stones, and all things beautiful, Lauren's artwork reflects her deep connection to the natural world. Over time, she has honed her skills with polymer clay, cultivating a style that is both distinctive and captivating. While she acknowledges there is always room for growth and refinement, Lauren is confident that her work possesses a unique identity.

With a desire to empower others to unleash their creativity, Lauren loves to share her artistic techniques and insights with aspiring makers. Through her creations, she hopes to inspire others to craft something truly magical and meaningful.

Index

windows and the fuselage re-contoured with area rule to reduce transonic drag. The F8U-1P then had its successful first flight, flown by test pilot John Konrad on December 17, 1956—the fifty-third anniversary of the Wright Brothers' original flight at Kill Devil Hills in North Carolina.

With the defense-wide aircraft naming standard adopted in 1962, the F8U-1P became the RF-8A. The RF-8A was the first Crusader version to be inducted into a refurbishment and modernization program in 1965, in which seventy-three RF-8As received new wings with hardpoints for fuel drop tanks, and ventral fins for high-speed directional stability. With a boost in available electrical power, additional camera configurations could now also be mounted. Beginning in 1977, a second upgrade of the RF-8G was carried out. Many of the J-57-P-22 engines of the RF-8Gs were replaced by more powerful J57-P-429 engines. New electrical wiring was provided and new electronic countermeasures equipment was added. These modified RF-8Gs could be identified by the presence of two large afterburner cooling air intakes mounted on their upper tail cones. The last active-duty RF-8Gs flew with Navy Light Photographic Squadron 63 (VFP-63) until 1982. But the RF-8G continued on in the Navy Reserve, flying until 1987 with VFP-206 stationed at Naval Air Facility Andrews. The Smithsonian's RF-8G was the last aircraft to fly with VFP-206. On the day after its last flight, it was delivered to the museum.

The Steven F. Udvar-Hazy Center's Crusader, Bureau Number 146860, was initially delivered to the Navy as an F8U-1P, and spent its first ten years in operational service with the Marine Corps, flying with VMCJ-3 at Marine Corps Air Station El Toro California, and with VCMJ-1 flying 200 combat hours in Southeast Asia. In 1969 it was converted to an RF-8G model and assigned to VFP-63 at Naval Air Station Miramar, from where it made another combat cruise aboard USS *Hancock* in 1970 and 1971, logging another 200 hours of combat over North Vietnam. On return from its 1971 cruise, it was stored briefly at Davis-Monthan Air Force Base until assigned to VFP-206 at Joint Base Andrews-Naval Air Facility Washington (NAF Andrews). It was the last aircraft to fly with VFP-206. Over its lifetime this aircraft has had 11 overhauls, 260 operational service months, almost 22 operational years, and a total of 28 years of naval service. Its record of 7,475 total flight hours is more than that of any other Crusader in history. During its career it made a total of 8,896 landings, 689 carrier arrestments, and 714 catapult shots. Its last carrier landing was in October 1986, and it made its last flight in March

THE VOUGHT F8U CRUSADER AT THE SMITHSONIAN NATIONAL AIR AND SPACE MUSEUM

The aircraft that would emerge from the U.S. Navy's Carrier-based Supersonic Day Fighter study in the early 1950s was the F8U Crusader, an innovative swept-wing supersonic design powered by the new Pratt & Whitney J57 turbojet engine. It would achieve an outstanding record throughout its service life, in primarily two versions: the cannon-equipped gunfighter and the camera-equipped photo-reconnaissance airplane. It earned for the Navy and Chance Vought, its designer and manufacturer, a joint award of the Collier Trophy for the conception, design, and development of the first carrier-based aircraft to exceed 1,000 mph. It set the first national speed record of more than 1,000 mph to win for the U.S. Navy its first Thompson Trophy. And it was the first aircraft to fly across the United States faster than the speed of sound.

Of the 1,261 F-8s that were built, 144 photo-reconnaissance versions were authorized early in the production program. Those F8U-1Ps differed from the standard F8U-1 in having the four 20mm cannons replaced with topographic mapping cameras, the ammunition compartment replaced with a night-photo flare package, the underside reshaped to accommodate camera

(All photos courtesy of the Smithsonian National Air and Space Museum)

"Raymond A. Boyd, Cdr., USN." *U.S. Naval Academy Virtual Memorial Hall*, accessed 19 July 2024, https://usnamemorialhall.org/index.php/RAYMOND_A._BOYD,_CDR,_USN.

Riera, Robert E., Rear Admiral, USN. *F-8 Tactical Manual*. NAVAIR 01-45HHA-1T. Naval Air Systems Command, 1 July 1969.

Riley, Tad, Lieutenant Commander, USN. Interview by Rear Adm. Paul Gillcrist [1995].

Rodgers, George F., Commander, USN, ed. "Bullet Sets Two Records." *Naval Aviation News* (October 1957). Accessed at https://www.history.navy.mil/content/dam/nhhc/research/histories/naval-aviation/Naval%20Aviation%20News/1950/pdf/oct57.pdf.

———. "Collier Trophy Goes to F8U." *Naval Aviation News* (January 1958), https://www.history.navy.mil/research/histories/.

———. "Crusader Squadrons Join Fleet." *Naval Aviation News* (January 1958), https://www.history.navy.mil/research/histories/.

———. "Drafting Board to Mothballs." *Naval Aviation News* (September 1957), https://www.history.navy.mil/research/histories/.

Shea, Joseph. Interview by Ernest Snowden, 18 June 2024.

Smith, Kevin M., Captain, USN (Ret.). *The Sonic Warrior: Chronicles of a TOPGUN Pioneer*. Redemption, 2022.

Spangenberg, George. Interview by Capt. Rosario Rausa, USN (Ret.), September 1989. Oral History Project, National Naval Aviation Museum, accessed at http://aviationarchives.blogspot.com/2018/02/george-spangenberg-oral-history.html.

Spidle, William D. *Vought F-8 Crusader*. Specialty, 2017.

Switzer, William "Striker," Captain, USN (Ret.). Interview by Ernest Snowden, 30 May 2024.

Thomason, Tommy. *Vought F8U-3 Crusader III: Super Crusader*. Steve Ginter, 2010.

Tillman, Barrett. *MiG Master: The Story of the F-8 Crusader*. Nautical and Aviation, 1980.

———. "F8U-1T (V-408) Detail Specification," 12 October 1955. National Archives and Records Administration, College Park, MD.

———. "F8U-3 (V-401) Design Philosophy: Engineering Report 9874," 7 October 1955. National Archives and Records Administration, College Park, MD.

———. "F8U-3 Detail Specification," 12 October 1955. National Archives and Records Administration, College Park, MD.

———. "First Class Completes 'Post Grad Course'" (LTV Aerospace Corporation, Dallas, TX), *Crusader Fighter Report* 3, no. 2. (February 1969), http://f8crusader.org/LTV_CFR/LTV%20Crusader%20Fighter%20Report%201969%20Vol.%203.pdf.

———. "Guide to F8U-3 Mock-Up," 12 October 1955. National Archives and Records Administration, College Park, MD.

———. "Gunfighters on Target." (LTV Aerospace Corporation, Dallas, TX) *Crusader Fighter Report* 3, no. 1 (January 1969). Accessed at https://www.f8crusader.org/LTV_CFR/LTV%20Crusader%20Fighter%20Report%201969%20Vol.%203.pdf.

———. "Navy Day Fighter Design Philosophy: Report 8699," 21 February 1953. Vought Aircraft Company Collection, University of Texas at Dallas.

———. "Performance Data, Navy Day Fighter (OS-130): Report 8702," 26 February 1953. Vought Aircraft Company Collection, University of Texas at Dallas.

———. "Post-Graduate Courses Continue." (LTV Aerospace Corporation, Dallas, TX), *Crusader Fighter Report* 4, no. 1 (January 1970). Accessed at https://www.f8crusader.org/LTV_CFR/LTV%20Crusader%20Fighter%20Report%201970%20Vol.%204.pdf.

———. "Proposal Detail Specification: Navy Day Fighter (OS-130): Report 8978," 3 June 1953. Vought Aircraft Company Collection, University of Texas at Dallas.

———. "Standard Aircraft Characteristics: V-383 Day Fighter: Report 8700," 25 February 1953. Vought Aircraft Company Collection, University of Texas at Dallas.

———. "V-401 Project Philosophy and Plan," 19 January 1956. Vought Aircraft Company Collection, University of Texas at Dallas.

———. "VF-62 Pilots Boost Flight Totals." (LTV Aerospace Corporation, Dallas, TX), *Crusader Fighter Report* 3, no. 1 (January 1969). Accessed at https://www.f8crusader.org/LTV_CFR/LTV%20Crusader%20Fighter%20Report%201969%20Vol.%203.pdf.

———. "XF8U-1 & F8U-1 Program Synopsis: July 1952: December 1956," 1957. Vought Aircraft Company Collection, University of Texas at Dallas.

Weaver, Michael. "An Examination of the F-8 Crusader through Archival Sources." (Royal Aeronautical Society, London, U.K.) *Journal of Aeronautical History* (2018).

Welch, J. Michael, Captain, USN (Ret.). Interview by Ernest Snowden, 2 July 2024.

Windsor, Robert W. "Duke," Captain, USN (Ret.). Interview by Donald R. Lennon, 6 February 1988. Oral History Project OH0107, East Carolina University, accessed at https://digital.lib.ecu.edu/special/ead/findingaids/oh0107?q=Windsor.

Wood, Phil, Captain, USN (Ret.), with Wally Schirra and Zeke Cormier. *Wildcats to Tomcats*. Phalanx, 1995.

Woodford, Thomas R. "Have Drill/Have Ferry Tactical Evaluation." National Air and Space Intelligence Center, April 1970, accessed 19 July 2024 at https://nsarchive2.gwu.edu/NSAEBB/NSAEBB443/docs/area51_51.PDF.

Hobart, Vernon B. "CVA Marks 'Forty Years of Firsts.'" (Chance Vought Aircraft, Dallas, TX), *Vought Vanguard*, 8 November 1957. Vought Aircraft Company Collection, University of Texas at Dallas.

———. "F8U-1 Is Named Crusader." (Chance Vought Aircraft, Dallas, TX), *Chance Vought News*, August 1955. Vought Aircraft Company Collection, University of Texas at Dallas.

———. "F8U Smashes Coast-to-Coast Record." (Chance Vought Aircraft, Dallas, TX), *Vought Vanguard*, 17 July 1957. Vought Aircraft Company Collection, University of Texas at Dallas.

———. "Navy Unveils Day Fighter." (Chance Vought Aircraft, Dallas, TX), *Chance Vought News*, 20 June 1955. Vought Aircraft Company Collection, University of Texas at Dallas.

Hobson, Chris. *Vietnam Air Losses*. Midland, 2001.

Hyland, John J., Admiral, USN. "U.S. Air-to-Air Activity in Southeast Asia: July to December 1967, Staff Study 9-68. Commander-in-Chief U.S. Pacific Fleet, Pearl Harbor, HI, 31 August 1968. Naval History and Heritage Command.

Jack, Kenneth V. *Eyes of the Fleet over Vietnam*. Casemate, 2021.

Kastner, T. M., Commander, USN. "The Navy Preliminary Evaluation: Its Role in the Development of Naval Aircraft." AIAA Conference Paper. American Institute of Aeronautics and Astronautics, 25 March 1968, accessed at https://arc.aiaa.org/doi/abs/10.2514/6.1968-265.

Kinsley, William A., Commander, USN. "Crusaders Now with VX-3." *Naval Aviation News* (March 1957), https://www.history.navy.mil/research/histories/.

———. "F8U Stars in FIP Program." *Naval Aviation News* (April 1957), https://www.history.navy.mil/research/histories/.

———. "F8U Wins Thompson Trophy." *Naval Aviation News* (October 1956), https://www.history.navy.mil/research/histories/.

———. "Navy Planes Span Nation." *Naval Aviation News* (August 1957), https://www.history.navy.mil/research/histories/.

———. "VF-32 Pilots Fly the F8U." *Naval Aviation News* (July 1957), https://www.history.navy.mil/research/histories/.

Klusmann, Charles, Captain, USN (Ret.). Interview by Ernest Snowden, 30 April 2024.

Lawrence, William P., Vice Admiral, USN (Ret.). Interview by Paul Stillwell, 24 September 1990. Oral History Program, U.S. Naval Institute photo archive.

Levinson, Jeffrey L. *Alpha Strike Vietnam: The Navy's Air War, 1964 to 1973*. Presidio, 1989.

Linnekin, Richard, Captain, USN (Ret.). *Eighty Knots to Mach 2*. Naval Institute Press, 1991.

Loftin, E. H., Commander, USN. "Commanding Officer's Endorsement." Memorandum EHL: Ins 5800 Ser: 778, 9 November 1961, National Naval Aviation Museum Archive.

Mallick, Donald. *The Smell of Kerosene: A Test Pilot's Odyssey*. National Aeronautics and Space Administration, 2003.

Marinshaw, Steve "SAM," Commander, USN (Ret.). Interview by Ernest Snowden, 1 April 2024.

Marolda, Edward J. "Survival, Evasion, Resistance & Escape." *Naval History* Magazine (April 2024), accessed June 2024 at https://www.usni.org/magazines/naval-history-magazine/2024/april/survival-evasion-resistance-escape.

Mersky, Peter, Commander, USN (Ret.). *F-8 Crusader Units of the Vietnam War*. Osprey, 1998.

———. *F-8 Crusader vs. MiG-17*. Osprey, 2014.

———. *RF-8 Crusader Units over Cuba and Vietnam*. Osprey, 1999.

———. "The Last Launch." *Naval Aviation News*. (July/August 1987), https://www.history.navy.mil/research/histories/.

———. *U.S. Marine Corps Aviation Since 1912*. Naval Institute Press, 2009.

Miottel, Robert "Crash." Interview by Ernest Snowden, 1 April 2024.

National Aeronautics Association. "The Collier Trophy," accessed 19 July 2024 at https://naa.aero/awards/awards-trophies/collier-trophy/.

Nichols, John B., Commander, USN (Ret.), with Barrett Tillman. *On Yankee Station*. Naval Institute Press, 1987.

Pace, Steve. *Vought's F-8 Crusader: Development and Testing, Foreign Users and F8U-3*. Steve Ginter, 1988.

Pearson, Larry "Hoss," Captain, USN (Ret.). Interview by Ernest Snowden, 5 June 2024.

Pedersen, Dan. *Top Gun: An American Story*. Hachette Books, 2019

Peña, Fabio. "USS *Franklin D. Roosevelt* (CVA-42)." *NavSource Online: Aircraft Carrier Photo Archive*, accessed 19 July 2024 at https://www.navsource.org/archives/02/cv-42/42m.htm.

Poock, G. K. "Trends in Major Aircraft Accident Rates." Naval Postgraduate School, Monterey, CA, June 1976, accessed 19 July 2024 at https://apps.dtic.mil/sti/tr/pdf/ADA027256.pdf.

Poole, Walter S. *The Joint Chiefs of Staff and National Policy*. Office of the Chairman of the Joint Chiefs, 2011, accessed 15 June 2024 at https://www.jcs.mil/Portals/36/Documents/History/Policy/Policy_V008.pdf.

Rasmussen, Robert "Raz," Captain, USN (Ret.). Interview by Ernest Snowden, 7 May 2024.